Surprise in the Mountains

Surprise in the Mountains

by Natalie Savage Carlson

illustrations by Elise Primavera

Harper & Row, Publishers

Other Books by Natalie Savage Carlson

The Family Under the Bridge

A Grandmother for the Orphelines

Luvvy and the Girls

The Talking Cat and other stories of French Canada

The Tomahawk Family

Surprise in the Mountains
Text copyright © 1983 by Natalie Savage Carlson
Illustrations copyright © 1983 by Elise Primavera
All rights reserved.
Printed in the United States of America.

Library of Congress Cataloging in Publication Data
Carlson, Natalie Savage.
  Surprise in the mountains.

  Summary: Old Quill, a prospector, finds a special
present under his tree on Christmas morning.
  [1. Christmas—Fiction.   2. Animals—Fiction]
I. Primavera, Elise, ill.   II. Title.
PZ7.C2167Su 1983   [E]   82-47716
ISBN 0-06-021008-7
ISBN 0-06-021009-5 (lib. bdg.)

First Edition
Designed by Al Cetta
1 2 3 4 5 6 7 8 9 10

Especially for Mari,
Michelle,
and Timothy Mortimer.

Mountain men of the old west said that once each night every wild creature stirred at the same moment. And it made a rustle that broke the stillness of the sierras.

Old Quill, the grizzled prospector, heard it every night.

Perhaps the deer tossed his antlers.

Perhaps the jaybird raised his feathered crest.

Perhaps the bobcat licked her spotted fur, and the ringtail cat clawed the bark.

The mountain men did not know why this happened.

But Old Quill did.

"They're just lettin' me know they're all around," he said to his burro, Shag. "So I won't feel lonesome in the dark."

He talked to Shag because there was no one else to talk to.

Old Quill always woke early and went to work. He panned the creeks to find gold dust to buy his few needs. And as he walked with Shag, he picked up any feathers in his path. He carefully put them into a pocket. They were blue feathers of the jaybird. Red of the woodpecker. Yellow of the lark.

"Gifts from my bird friends," he told Shag. "Ain't that so, old-timer?"

The burro waggled his long ears.

"You think so too," said the old man.

While sitting by the fire at his campsites, Old Quill often saw eyes glowing in the dark. They were the green glow of the bobcat. Red of the jackrabbit. Blue of the deer.

"Keepin' me company," he told Shag.

The burro pawed the ground.

"Knew you'd understand," said Old Quill.

When winter came to the sierras, Old Quill worried about the wild creatures.

So he scattered oats for the hungry birds and rabbits, and wisps of hay for the deer and mice.

He threw bits of his own hard biscuit and dried beef in the snow for the foxes and pack rats and raccoons.

"A purty sight, all this white," he said to his burro. "But a bad time for the wild critters and us too. How much longer will our vittles last? And how can I buy more at the tradin' post since my gold dust is all used up? Can't work frozen cricks now."

The burro snuffled.

"So you know we're in a bad way too," said Old Quill.

The track of a fox through the snow led the prospector to an abandoned miner's cabin near a cave.

"We'll hole up here for Christmas," Old Quill told his burro, "since the fox invited us. If I take the shack, will the cave suit you?"

Shag switched his frayed tail.

"Knew you'd be satisfied," said the old man. "It's a spell since we've had such shelter. That fox was tryin' to help us."

He led Shag into the cave at sundown. By lantern light he studied the gouges and scratches in its walls.

"Hoped to make his fortune here, I reckon," he said of the departed miner. "I was like him when I was younger. Dug the earth and clawed the dirt. Hopin' to find the big vein of gold. 'Twas just greed, pardner.

Now I'm content to work the cricks even if the find is skimpy. Don't you think that's best, Shag?"

The burro wiggled his soft lips.

"Knew you'd agree," said Old Quill.

He remembered to scatter some hard biscuit bits over the snow when he returned to the cabin.

Old Quill wearily stretched himself out on the hard bunk. He pulled a mangy buffalo robe over himself and sighed deeply. As he lay there, he heard the stir of the wild ones.

Perhaps the marmot was curling tighter into his long sleep.

Perhaps the raven was pulling his wings closer against the chill.

Perhaps the bighorn was pawing the icy crust, and the wolf's tail was brushing the snow.

"They're tellin' me not to worry," mumbled Old Quill. "If they can make it through the winter on empty bellies, so can I."

Next morning, he woke early and went to the cave with his lantern.

"Christmas is almost here," he told the burro. "Long as we have shelter, we must get ready for it. Got to fetch a tree and pretty it up. You want to come help me?"

Shag pulled at his hobbles.

"Knew you'd be willin'," said Old Quill.

He patted the burro's shaggy neck, then untied the hobbles. He led him down the trail until he saw just the right fir, small but bushy, growing all by itself on the mountainside. He chopped it down and lashed it to Shag's back.

Old Quill brought the tree to the cabin and set it on the box beside the bunk. Then, having no tinsel or colored balls, he pulled the bird feathers from his pocket. He tied the blue of the jay, red of the woodpecker, and yellow of the lark into the branches of the little tree.

"Trimmed with gifts from my friends," he said.

Christmas Eve was as still as the other nights. Even the pack rat roving the hillside moved silently as falling snow.

He set out for the miner's cabin, where he had feasted on hard biscuit scraps the night before. Such were always good places for bits of glass or cuttings of tin. He hoped to make a good trade for the picking he had found in a snowslide.

The rat followed the chilly breeze through the big crack in the door. His beady eyes saw the tree on the box. He climbed to it while Old Quill lay still as a marmot himself.

The pack rat dropped his picking under the tree. He pulled a woodpecker feather from a branch and scurried away.

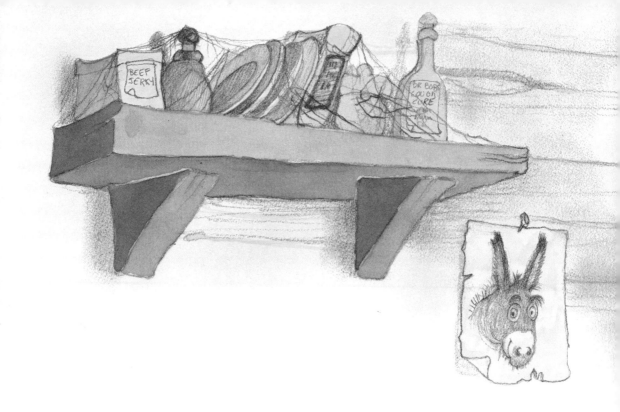

That morning, Old Quill woke early and pushed back the buffalo robe.

"Got to wish Shag a merry Christmas," he said.

He climbed from the bunk in his long gray underwear. His eyes turned to the tree. Then he saw something bright under its branches. It was the trade made by the pack rat.

The old man picked it up. He stared at it like a gray squirrel puzzled by a strange nut.

Then he whooped, "Wal, I'll be a porkypine's uncle if it ain't a gold nugget! But how did it get under my tree?"

Old Quill hastily pulled on his trousers and sheep-skin jacket. His hands trembled as he lit the wick of the lantern. Then he headed for the door with the nugget in his other hand.

"Got to show this to Shag," he declared.

Outside, he stopped and studied the feathery tracks in the snow about his doorway.

"Wal, I'll be a spider's granddaddy if it ain't a pack rat left me this gold," he declared.

He hurried to the cave.

"Merry Christmas, old-timer!" he greeted his burro.

He held up the nugget. "See? We got a Christmas gift from a grateful pack rat. It will last us till spring thaws the cricks. Now all of us will have a bite to eat once we've dropped in at the tradin' post."

"Hee-haw!" brayed the burro. "Hee-haw!"

"Knew you'd have somethin' to say about that," said Old Quill.